CW00763349

IMAGES OF ENGLAND

CENTRAL DONCASTER

IMAGES OF ENGLAND

CENTRAL DONCASTER

PETER TUFFREY

TEMPUS

For Albert Tuffrey, who initially inspired my interest in local history

Frontispiece: A scene on the southern side of the Market Place c.1900. Included in the row of properties at the rear are the two public houses the Black Swan and the Market Inn.

First published 1995
New edition 2003

Tempus Publishing Limited
The Mill, Brimscombe Port,
Stroud, Gloucestershire, GL5 2QG

British Library Cataloguing in Publication Data.
A catalogue record for this book is available from the British Library.

ISBN 0 7524 3016 5

Typesetting and origination by Tempus Publishing Limited
Printed in Great Britain by Midway Colour Print, Wiltshire

Contents

High Street looking north.

Introduction

Quite a number of Old Doncaster picture books have appeared over the last decade. So, in compiling this one, I have tried to choose images which have not been widely seen or illustrated before. The fascination of seeing how areas once looked and comparing them with their current appearance was how I first became hooked on old photographs. I'm sure many other people have gained an interest in the same way. The ones chosen for inclusion here will provide many moments of fascination and opportunities for making then and now comparisons.

The pictures cover the period from c.1890 to the present day. Well known local photographers such as Luke Bagshaw and Edgar Leonard Scrivens are featured. There are even some 'old' ones which I have taken myself, underlining that change is still a continual process in Doncaster.

The contents illustrate some of the points mentioned later in this introduction. In particular, the aerial views show how the town's layout has altered. The yards remind us of how appalling our living conditions once were. The redevelopment section illustrates a number of today's familiar features under construction and once well known landmarks being demolished.

I tend to feel that many locals assume that the only period in which Doncaster was drastically altered was during the 1960s. The truth is that every decade over the last century has brought changes although, admittedly, the intensity to which it has occurred over the last 35 years has probably not been rivalled before.

Perhaps an obvious starting point, to briefly outline some of these changes, would be the mid-19th century. This was when the railways came to Doncaster. Vast areas of land beyond the town's medieval core were sold to accommodate the influx of workers at the Great Northern Railway Company's Plant Works.

Thoroughfares like Camden Street, Bentinck Street and Catherine Street were built and Doncaster started to look like every other industrial town with rows and rows of terraced properties, a sprinkling of corner shops, pubs and places of worship.

The railway station was erected on the town's western side, and a splendid thoroughfare, perhaps aptly titled Station Road, provided access to and from the town centre. The buildings erected along Station Road were some of the most splendid ever seen in the town and included the Co-op Store, Glyn Hotel and Oriental Chambers.

Towards the turn of the century, Public Health Acts, indirectly, began to alter the town's appearance, as streets were widened to comply with them. Amongst the routes affected by the work were Baxter Gate, Sunny Bar, Cleveland Street, West Street, Silver Street, St Sepulchre Gate and Scot Lane.

These improvements were carried out by the Doncaster Corporation who were also responsible for a number of other projects: Grey Friars Road was established, a tramway system was opened, the cattle market was extended and the River Cheswold was culverted. Perhaps the Corporation's most ambitious and worthwhile project during the century's first decade was the building of North Bridge to replace the troublesome railway level crossing.

In the first quarter of the present century, the sinking of new pits and the laying of new railways to and from the workings presented a scene of activity probably unrivalled, for a town the size of Doncaster, anywhere else in the country. The principal new colleries were Armthorpe, Barnburgh, Bentley, Brodsworth, Bullcroft, Edlington, Hatfield, Hickleton, Maltby, Rossington and Thorne.

This meant that Doncaster, instead of being encircled by a purely pastoral countryside, was surrounded by a busy mining area, thickly populated, producing millions of tons of coal and adding enormously to the wealth of the nation.

Also, in the commercial field, many new firms were established, not only in the town centre, but in the outlying areas, particularly on the Wheatley Estate, extending in a north-easterly direction along the River Don. Amongst these were British Bemberg, Crompton Parkinson Ltd and the International Harvester Company of Great Britain. Wheatley was one of many local estates which were broken up, others included Carr House and Sprotbrough.

During the Second World War, in three of the most serious air raids experienced in the Doncaster District about 39 people lost their lives and more than 50 were seriously injured. The first to cause fatalities was on a Saturday evening in December 1940, and was thought to have been caused by a lone raider attracted to the town by a fire. Small calibre bombs were dropped across country from Wadworth to Edlington and larger ones at the Barnsley Road/York Road junction near the Sun Inn. Others fell a short distance away in the thickly populated Bentley West End area.

In the post-War years, the Council produced a Development Plan which was approved by the Minister of Housing and Local Government in 1953. The Plan was to control the town's major lines of development for the next 20 years. The main features included making the town centre a commercial and business area, constructing new roads, and establishing industrial estates.

In the 1960s, central Doncaster witnessed rampant redevelopment as the aims of the Development Plan were carried out. Consequently, new roads have now been established and much of the 19th century housing, dating from the town's first industrial expansion, has been cleared.

As the 21st century approaches, small scale developments are still taking place within the town centre. At the time of writing, a new massive office block is under construction in Wood Street. But, even greater ones are occurring on the outskirts. The rail port is now well under way and the second phase of the Dome Leisure Park development promises to be a very exciting project.

In fact, the mood for change and desire for civic pride is as strong now as it ever was in the past. This will obviously provide much source material for authors, comparable to myself, in the next century.

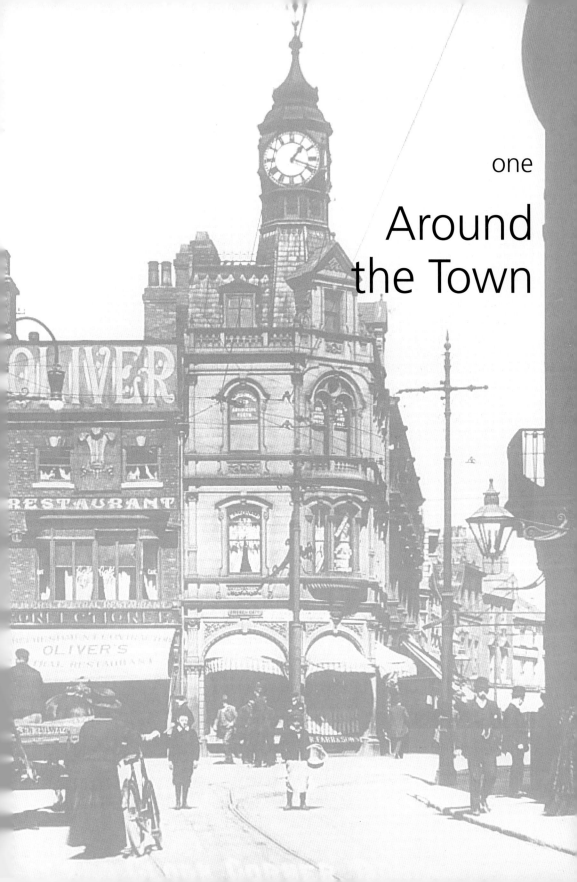

one

Around
the Town

North Bridge looking towards the town centre.

The widening of Baxter Gate during the early 1890s included the demolition of a site at the junction of French Gate/Baxter Gate, commonly known as Clock Corner. During 1895 new, more elegant premises, housing a clock tower, were constructed to the designs of architect J.G. Walker.

St Sepulchre Gate c.1905, before street widening commenced c.1912.

Marsh Gate looking north c.1905. The New River Tavern is on the left.

The Silver Street/Hall Gate corner before the ramshackle building in the centre – occupied by tobacconist Daniel Portergill – was demolished in 1912 for the construction of the Prudential Building. The latter was erected to the design of Paul Waterhouse, a President of the Royal Institute of British Architects.

High Street looking north. Featured on the left are the premises of house furnishers Sheard, Binnington & Co., and the Mansion House. The boy on the extreme right is standing outside J.G. Timmins & Co's tobacconist shop. Next door is the imposing frontage of the Lyceum Restaurant, once the 'Victoria Rooms'.

Baxter Gate during street widening c.1893. The Clock Corner and the business premises of bookseller and printer E.G. Bisat and boot-and-shoe maker Frederick White – seen here on the thoroughfare's northern side – were amongst the properties demolished for the work to be carried out.

The junction of St Sepulchre Gate/St Swithin's Terrace, as seen from Balby Bridge. Much of the property depicted, built during the late 19th century, was cleared as a result of several Compulsory Purchase Orders during the 1960s. The Balby Bridge fly-over, constructed during the mid-1970s, now covers much of the site. This provides access to the M18 motorway and the southern relief route.

Printing Office Street from Station Road. The Public Benefit Boot Co. Ltd's building on the left was erected around 1899. Before the work took place, Doncaster Corporation set back the street line which was very narrow at this point. Trams working on the Racecourse route used Printing Office Street as part of a relief route when coping with the large crowds at race-meetings. The premises occupied by grocers Sanderson & Son on the right were demolished, along with several others, during the late 1930s to facilitate the construction of the Co-operative Emporium, designed by local architects T.H. Johnson & Son, and now known as the Danum Store.

The Hall Gate/South Parade junction looking north. The property on the right containing private residences has since been converted for commercial use. The garage (left), once occupied by R. Lambert, was demolished to facilitate the widening of Branson Street, now merged with Waterdale.

The Hall Gate/High Street junction, looking north, in the days when traffic congestion was non-existent at this point and a 'bobby' could quite easily control the flow of vehicles. One of the most noted buildings in the picture is the Reindeer Hotel (left) dating from at least 1782. Since being demolished in 1962 many people have lamented its demise, and criticised the new characterless buildings erected on the site.

E.L.S. I-258. The New Bridge, Doncaster.

In 1907, Doncaster Corporation formed a special committee to eliminate the nuisance and delay of the Marsh Gate railway crossing. Subsequent discussions with the Great Northern Railway Co. resulted in the proposal to construct a bridge over the railway line. Work began in 1908. The bridge's designer was Edward Parry, an eminent engineer, whilst the construction work was carried out by local firm H. Arnold & Son.

E.L.S.S. Opening Of The New Bridge At Doncaster. Feb. 11th 1910.
Coun. G. Smith Calls For Three Cheers For The Mayor.

The New Bridge was formally opened by Alderman J.F. Clark J.P. The estimated expenditure laid before Parliament by the Corporation's Engineers, including land, buildings and works was £116,662 and the borrowing powers asked for and obtained were for a sum of £80,000 for the Bridge works, and £5,000 for the tramway thereon, the difference of £31,662 being made up by the substantial contribution of the G.N.R.

The Cleveland Street/Printing Office Street junction viewed from Young Street. The Lord Nelson public house, dating from 1870 and formerly known as the Old Brewery Tavern, dominates the centre of picture. The building was set back in 1934 to facilitate the widening of Cleveland Street, and is currently titled 'Nelsons'. The gate on the right led to property known as High Street Buildings. This was cleared around 1924 and York House erected.

St Sepulchre Gate looking west. On the left, the business premises include those of furniture and bedding specialists Wagstaff's, and fishmongers and fruiterers Scarborough Bros. The photograph was probably taken c.1908 just before West Street (right) was widened. As a result the Leopard Hotel was set back. The tram in the distance is travelling to, or returning from, Balby or Hexthorpe, as part of the routes ran along this section of St Sepulchre Gate.

Carr House Road, Hyde Park, from near the junction with Elmfield Road. Initially, the Hyde Park trams, which started running in 1902, terminated at Jarratt Street. A year later, with the construction of new streets, the line was extended to Chequer Road. All the houses on the right have since been demolished for the construction of the southern relief route.

St Sepulchre Gate looking towards the town centre, from a position near the Horse and Jockey pub. Horse-drawn traffic seemingly dominates the street during a break in tram traffic. The gateway on the left belongs to St Thomas' Hospital. This has since been moved to a site near the Chequer Road Museum & Art Gallery.

The Spring Gardens/St Sepulchre Gate junction looking south. Trams bound for Hyde Park left St Sepulchre Gate at this point. The corner site, behind the figures in the foreground, is captured prior to redevelopment and was eventually occupied for a number of years by drapers W. Elland & Sons.

St Sepulchre Gate near the Red House corner, looking towards the town centre. The corner was set back in the 1920s and then became known as Jacobs' Corner after house furnisher Harry Jacobs who had a shop within the new complex of buildings erected on the site. R. Pillin Jnr's pianoforte warehouse is on the right.

Silver Street, with Sunny Bar in the distance, is depicted c.1915, a few years after the northern side (left) was set back. The tall buildings on the right include the St Leger Tavern, Palace Buffet and Palace Theatre (later Essoldo Cinema). The Buffet and Cinema were demolished in the 1960s.

St Sepulchre Gate taken from the junction with Station Road. Interestingly, when car no. 6 was purchased, along with 14 others, by Doncaster Corporation in 1902, it did not have a top deck cover. This was added in 1913, thus becoming known as a balcony car. The vehicle was withdrawn from service in 1930.

This is part of the area sometimes referred to as Town End. The Three Horse Shoes public house, in the distance, was rebuilt in 1914. Mill Bridge or St Mary's Bridge, reconstructed in 1899, is on the right. The building on the left was once occupied by motor body builder P.D. Warriner.

Held aloft in this procession moving south along Bennetthorpe is the banner of the Hoyland & Silkstone branch of the Yorkshire Miners' Association. Noted on the right are the premises of cycle makers W.E. Clark & Co. who also had another outlet in Station Road. To the left, the Rockingham Inn offers 'good stabling'.

Much of this area at the Cleveland Street/High Street junction is presently occupied by the Danum Hotel. The latter replaced the Ram Hotel which was demolished around 1908 and the site set back for the widening of Cleveland Street. At one time, the Reindeer Vaults (out of view) stood on the opposite side of the road.

St Sepulchre Gate from near the Spring Gardens junction, and facing the town centre. Properties on the left include the Good Woman public house, Crystal Palace beer house, and clothier, H.Lightowler's shop. Existing on the right are pawnbrokers, Millard Bros; butchers, Rhoden & Son; and fruiterer, G. Foster.

This is one of many Edwardian postcards which show processions and parades travelling along Hall Gate. Viewed from first floor balconies, these spectacles must have been very entertaining for residents. Sadly, Hall Gate is now a mere shadow of its former self, having endured many unsympathetic alterations.

French Gate and Clock Corner from High Street. The scaffolding (left) indicates that demolition work has begun on the Newsroom and Library (out of view) in St Sepulchre Gate. This was for the widening of the thoroughfare and the work continued through to the 1930s.

Car no.2, approaching the High Street/ Scot Lane corner, is working on the Racecourse route, which was opened on 30 June 1930. The route was 'single tracked' from Station Road to the Mansion House (left). From there however, the remainder of the route was 'double tracked'. Trolleybuses operated the service from 1930.

Beckett Road probably came into being during the early 1880s when landowner Major H. Browne decided to develop his Wheatley Estate. Intially, it extended from the Holmes to Avenue Road. Now, it stretches into Wheatley. Business premises on the left include those of plumber T. Reasbeck.

The junction of Nether Hall Road/Broxholme Lane, with Highfield Road stretching beyond. The Highfield Estate was advertised for sale in 1876 with lots suitable for the erection of villa and other residences. Highfield Road was laid out on the line of an old field path.

Apley Road, off Chequer Road, was built around 1892/3 by several builders including Reuben Moate & Sons; George Stevenson; Lamb & Patrick; and P. Crawley.

Privately-owned charabancs, like the one seen here in St Sepulchre Gate passing near the Horse and
Jockey pub, often competed fiercely for passengers alongside the Corporation's trams and motorbuses.
Scarborough Bros' four-gabled premises may be identified in the distance.

Looking along Broxholme Lane, once called Lime Lane, from the junction with Thorne Road. Houses
on the western side of the street (on the left here) between Nether Hall Road and Thorne Road were
designed around 1892 by F.W. Masters, who gave a distinctive character to them by using cream-
coloured bricks.

Bawtry Road, or a section of the Great North Road as it was once known, looking towards the town centre. The rural appearance gives an indication of how the area once looked to stage coach passengers. Today, a dual carriageway and a roundabout, providing access to the Dome Leisure Park, dominate the scene.

Jubilee Road, off Beckett Road, appears to have been laid out, and the houses built, between 1896 and 1904. Therefore, the road probably commemorates Queen Victoria's Jubilee of 1897.

St Sepulchre Gate west and the many retail outlets it once contained. Included in this section were cycle and gramophone dealers, Millns & Co. Note the tramway passing loop in the foreground.

Alderman Mark Dowson, besides holding public office, was a tailor and oufitter with premises in Hall Gate and Silver Street. His funeral procession is seen in Cleveland Street on 16 August 1909, passing the Salvation Army Hall and the gardens of High Street Buildings (out of view).

The Old Exchange Brewery Tavern and the Saracen's Head public house provide a backdrop for this picture taken from the Cleveland Street/Cartwright Street junction. Unfortunately, those posing are unidentified.

South Parade from Hall Gate. The Majestic cinema (left) had a relatively short life span. It opened in December, 1920 as the South Parade cinema, was re-styled the Majestic two years later, and demolished in 1933. The Gaumont (called the Odeon from 20 January 1987) was subsequently built on the site.

Street widening work is in progress at the Nether Hall Road-end of East Laith Gate during 1931. While some properties on the street's eastern side were demolished for the scheme, the Britannia Inn on the opposite side, at the Silver Street corner, was also cleared.

Photographer G. S. Sullivan was noted at 9a High Street in 1908. Between 1910 and 1944 his 'Don Studio' existed at the St Sepulchre Gate/Elsworth street corner. He took many pictures for the *Doncaster Gazette*.

The Hall Gate/Prince's Street corner captured in 1953 when a scheme existed to widen the latter thoroughfare. In the event the proposal was never carried out, and the property depicted is presently occupied by radio, television, video, and furniture dealers Barker & Wigfall.

Chaos was caused by extensive flooding in the Doncaster area during the early 1930s. The extent of the problem is seen here in Marsh Gate. The main buildings in the picture, the Bridge Hotel (centre), St Andrew's Church (in the distance), and the George and Dragon Hotel (right) have all been demolished.

Nether Hall Road c.1955 when trolleybuses operated along the thoroughfare, travelling to, or from, Beckett Road or Wheatley Hills. Doncaster's last trolleybus ran on the Beckett Road route on 14 December 1963.

Stott's Garage on Bawtry Road. This was demolished during the 1980s and a new structure erected.

This section of St Sepulchre Gate once provided the terminating point for a number of trolleybuses, including those working on the Racecourse, Beckett Road and Wheatley Hills services.

Marsh Gate bus stand provided services to Leeds. This ceased on 19 August 1967. The building in the background was formerly a lodging house. Currently, it is known as the Warehouse and provides entertainment at weekends for young people.

Barnsley Brewery Co.'s ales, popular amongst the town's drinkers for years, are advertised on a trolleybus, marooned on the section of St Sepulchre Gate between the Thatched House and Shakespeare's Head pubs.

A group of people are seen here in Scot Lane prior to boarding several Leon Motor Co. coaches.

Silver Street facing Sunny Bar. Buildings on the right include those of Alfred Hall Ltd (ironmongers), Arnold Drury (butcher) and Brighter Homes (Decorators). On the left is the rear entrance to the Old George Hotel.

Baker Street with the Waterdale bus station in the distance. The street was cleared during the 1960s as a result of several Compulsory Purchase Orders. The site is presently covered by the Waterdale (formerly Golden Acres) shopping centre.

A section of Silver Street's southern side. The centre building was formerly occupied by Anelay Bros' building firm. To the right is the Essoldo Cinema. Both structures were demolished in the 1960s.

The section of Spring Gardens extended between Cleveland Street and Waterdale. All the properties were cleared in the early 1960s. The public baths may be seen in the distance.

The derelict three-storeyed property in the centre once formed a part of Church Street, extending from High Fisher Gate. The tall chimney in the distance belonged to J. Clark & Son's tannery in Friendly Street.

Elsworth Street from St Sepulchre Gate, looking towards Green Dyke Lane. It was built in the 1860s by John Elsworth and cleared a century later.

Albert Street from St Sepulchre Gate, looking towards Green Dyke Lane. It was initially titled Elsworth Street, but was retitled in 1862 to commemorate Prince Albert, Queen Victoria's husband.

West Street from West Laith Gate, looking towards St Sepulchre Gate. At one time, extending from the street's western side was Moore's Place; from the opposite side St Peter's Square. Many of the buildings on the right were demolished during the early 1960s for the construction of a G.P.O sorting office.

Marsh Gate looking north and viewed from North Bridge. The building on the left was occupied by the New River Tavern until 1937, after which it became a cafe. The rows of houses were cleared around 1970.

Marsh Gate with St Andrew's Church off centre to the left, motor engineers Wortley Bros. premises to the right, and the power station to the rear. Not a single building in the photograph is extant today.

East Laith Gate, pictured c.1960 facing south, before a shopping precinct, incorporating a bowling alley, was built on the area to the left. Further, clearance work has since taken place on this stretch of the street, leaving the Horse and Groom (extreme left) as the only survivor from the time of the photograph.

Marsh Gate looking south. Before the North Bridge opened in 1910, Marsh Gate provided the main route into Doncaster. St Andrew's Church, built in 1867, is on the right and the lodging house, the only building surviving today, is on the opposite side.

Cemetery Road, extending from St James' Street to Green Dyke Lane, looking towards the town centre. The road was originally titled Carr Lane. Much of Cemetery Road was demolished between 1971 and 1973. The section which has survived is at the street's southern end and is now known as Milton Walk.

The Dockin Hill Tavern, Dockin Hill Road dated from at least 1858. A plan was submitted in 1938 to rebuild the premises but this was never carried out. It is pictured here shortly before closure on 7 February 1971.

Arthur Street, looking north towards Green Dyke Lane, was set out by William Marratt on 4 August, 1954. He christened it 'Arthur Street' in compliment to his son Richard Arthur Warsop Marratt. The Arthur Street properties were cleared as a result of the 1968 Hyde Park Compulsory Purchase Order.

Duke Street looking towards St Sepulchre Gate. Much of the street was cleared during the mid-1930s. It is seen here some twenty years later before development took place on the western side.

Cleveland Street at the junction with Baker Street. Following the clearance of this line of property, during the early 1960s, the A.B.C. cinema was built on part of the site. Whilst the Stamp Corner sign is being displayed on one of the buildings, it was at this time occupied by the Busy Bee company.

Stanley Street residents are pictured protesting over a proposal to demolish the street. However, this was in vain as it was cleared around 1974. Stanley Gardens now exists on part of the site.

Station Road and Factory Lane, with Trafford Street beyond, are seen from the staircase of the Co-op (now Danum Store) on St Sepulchre Gate. Station Road was formally opened on 31 August 1882, by Mayor Charles Verity and members of the Doncaster Corporation. The Doncaster Co-operative Society's Store (left) was built in 1897, the Grand Theatre and Glyn Temperance Hotel (centre) 1899 and 1890 respectively, and the Oriental Chambers in 1897. During the Second World War, Station Road witnessed enemy action. Two people were killed when bombs were dropped on the area; extensive damage was caused to Clark's premises. All the buildings, apart from the Grand Theatre, were cleared in Station Road to facilitate the second phase of the Arndale (now French Gate) Centre development. Hopefully, the Grand Theatre can survive to remind us of what was once a splendid thoroughfare.

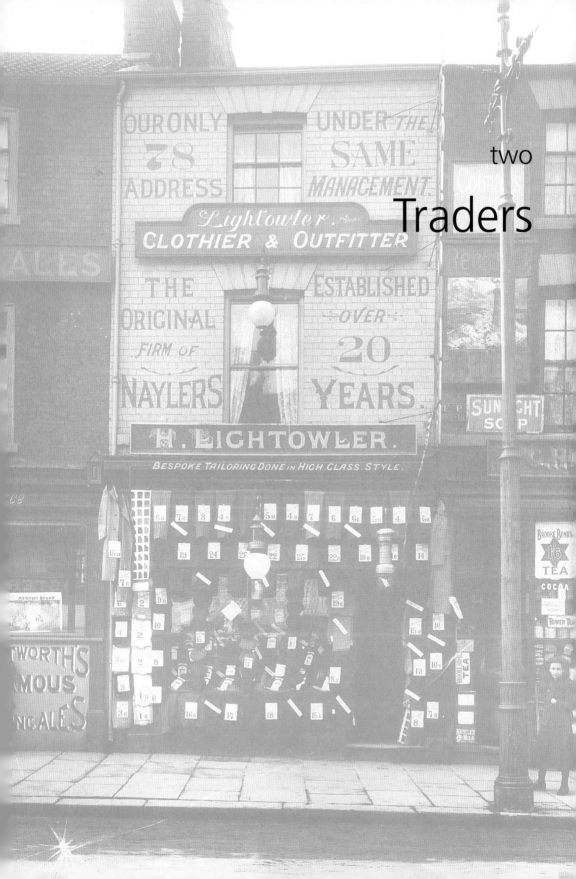

Arthur Bennett Dodds' cycle shop at 76 St Sepulchre Gate.

H. Lightowler was a native of Pontefract, where his father held the position of County Court bailiff. Having served an apprenticeship with a tailor and outfitter at Pontefract he came to Doncaster as an assistant in a St Sepulchre Gate business (pictured above) then carried on by Miss Naylor, who he married shortly afterwards. The turnover was mainly in workingmen's ready made clothing, but it also included a certain amount of items of a more expensive character. He opened a branch in Carr House Road, and later a business in high-class tailoring in Silver Street. The original business in St Sepulchre Gate was terminated by the disposal of the property at a price which Lightowler was not prepared to pay, and other businesses were either closed or disposed of. For the last few years of his life, his business was of a more casual character, for which he travelled the district. He died at the age of 60 in 1933. During his early life he was an ardent cyclist.

Right: Shoemaker and leather seller, Charles Gregory, outside his shop at number 86 St Sepulchre Gate. He was also a member of Doncaster Fire Brigade. After his death in 1917, the firm was continued by family members. In 1960, the firm moved to premises on the opposite side of the road, where it still thrives today.

Below: According to entries in *The Gazette Doncaster Directory & Yearbooks*, the Phoenix Firewood Co. or the Doncaster & District Firewood Co. only existed in Bentinck Street between 1909 and 1913.

J.R. Pearson's pawnbroker shop at 103a St Sepulchre Gate. Another pawnbroker, George Thompson, occupied the premises after Pearson. But, perhaps the building is best noted for accommodating the Railway Tavern, which was also known as the Bird in Hand or Punch Bowl. It existed between c.1844 and 1865. To the right is Portland Place. The old pub site and Portland Place were cleared for the construction of part of the Inner Relief Road.

Right: Drury & Co's drapery shop at 30 St Sepulchre Gate.

Below: Thomas William Draper's news agency and stationery shop at 22 Printing Office Street.

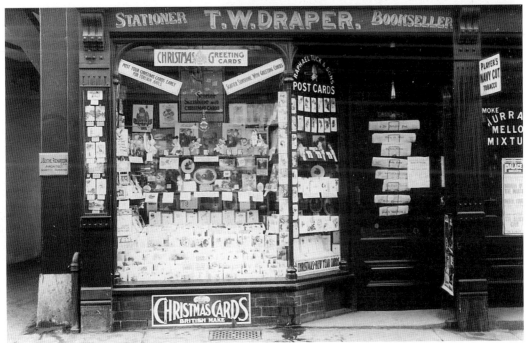

Butcher Hobson's shop on St Sepulchre Gate. After Hobson, another butcher occupied the premises. To the right is Arbitration Street.

Samuel Parkinson started his business in 1817 at 50-51 High Street, becoming known for his baking powder and butterscotch. Following Queen Victoria's visit to Doncaster in 1851, she gave exclusive permission to the firm to supply butterscotch to the Court. This was reciprocated by the Duchess of Kent on her visit a year later, and by the Princess of Wales in 1891.

Lumley & Postlethwaite established a furniture business at Retford in 1897. Two years later they opened a showroom in Doncaster's Oriental Chambers. In 1900, the pair rented 16 Hall Gate, pictured here.

Fruiterer T. Marshall's shop on St Sepulchre Gate.

Butcher J. Elvidge's shop at 153 St Sepulchre Gate.

Silver Street showing a paper hanger and decorator's shop and M.W. Pears' millinery shop. These properties were amongst those on the northern side which were demolished for the widening of the street.

Hincliffe & Allott's draper's shop at numbers 13 and 14 High Street.

This group of French Gate properties includes the business premises of Harry Wright (saddler); Charles Spittlehouse (hairdresser); and Thomas Smith (newsagent).

F.W. Strawson came to Doncaster from Lincolnshire in the early 1880s, and worked for E. Peniston & Co. He started his own business in 1905, in the premises shown here at Sunny Bar corner. This continued until his retirement to Worthing in 1936. He died six years later.

Jack Claybourn opened a bicycle and motorcycle shop in Askern c.1918. About 4 years later, he established a motor-garage. The business boomed and, in 1931, he moved to premises at the Hall Gate/Waterdale corner.

Millns & Co's cycle and gramophone dealers' shop at 92 and 94 St Sepulchre Gate. Later, the company occupied premises in High Street.

Reg Gray's radio and cycle shop at number 7 Printing Office Street.

Edwin White & Son's shop at number 71 French Gate. Edwin White was born in Baxter Gate in 1824. He was the eldest son of Charles White, stationer, who was, for a number of years, associated with Messrs Brooke and Hatfield in the ownership of the *Doncaster Gazette*. On the death of his father, Edwin succeeded to the business. Subsequently, the Baxter Gate premises were sold and Edwin removed the business to a shop in French Gate. Shortly after his son Herbert's death in 1907, he sold the French Gate premises to Messrs Boots Ltd. He never held any public office, his chief attention outside his business being devoted to the Doncaster Parish Church. He died in 1909.

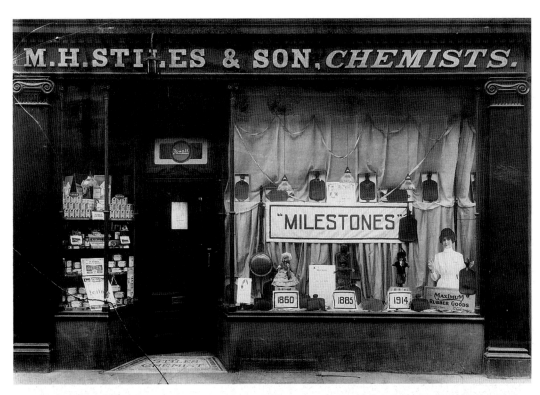

Mathew Henry Stiles & Son's shop in French Gate.

Left: Timber merchant, John Seth Trethewey's premises in Low Fisher Gate.

Below: Herbert Blamires established a wines and spirits shop on Beckett Road around 1922. Other shops were opened in Cleveland Street, as well as Huddersfield, Barnsley and Sheffield. After the War, only the Beckett Road shop was continued. When Herbert died in 1956, the business was run by his son Robert until his own death in 1972. Robert's wife Brenda continued the family tradition for another six years.

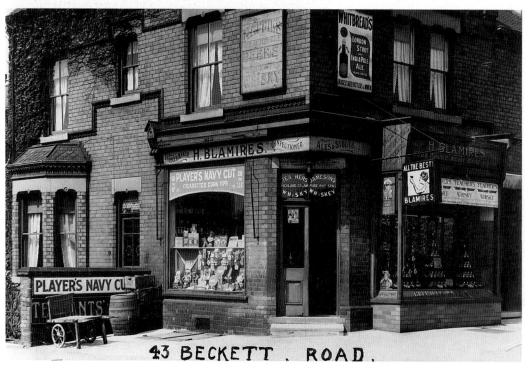

Barnsley-born William Porter, glass and china merchant, originally served his apprenticeship as a bricklayer. In 1872, his mother established the business of A. Porter & Sons at Barnsley. Around 1887, William moved to Doncaster and first opened a business at 68 French Gate, shown here.

Adjacent to noted wholesale confectioners, Parkinson & Son, at numbers 50 and 51 High Street, were the Borough Printing Works of Richard Henry Hepworth, at number 49.

Herbert Haresign, born in Lincolnshire, started in business as a fruiterer and florist in Spring Gardens during the late 1890s. In 1900, he moved to premises, depicted below, adjacent to the Ram Hotel. Eight years later he transferred to 36 and 37 High Street. Another move occurred in 1913 when the business transferred to 60 Hall Gate (left). These premises closed around 1924, and Herbert died in Sheffield, aged 84, in 1951.

Charles Brothers' ironmongers' business at 56 Market Place.

Fish and game dealer William Davy Borrill occupied premises at 17 St Sepulchre Gate and at 1 Copley
Road. Depicted here, c.1916, is the St Sepulchre Gate property being demolished to facilitate the setting
back of a section of the thoroughfare's southern side. Just visible, on the right, is part of the Elephant
Hotel, which had already been set back.

John Hastie, born in Northampton in 1846, lost an arm in 1865 whilst working in the Plant's Lower Turnery. He started a business in St Sepulchre Gate as a tobacconist and newsagent around 1870, but three years later purchased a drapery shop at 93 St Sepulchre Gate. Eventually another outlet was added in St Sepulchre Gate and one established in the Market Place. John Hastie died in 1913, the business being carried on by his two sons who opened other shops in High Street and Scot Lane. The business closed in 1953.

Westfield's removal business was started in Bentley during the late 1890s by Sam Westfield, a native of Lincolnshire. During 1933, the firm moved to York Road and remained a family run concern until being sold in 1988 by Sam's grandson, Alan Westfield.

Richard Hodgson and Richard Hepworth's St Sepulchre Gate grocery business was established in 1872. Both men had previous retailing experience. Hodgson as a tobacconist, Hepworth as a provision's dealer.

Fishmonger, Joseph Wilkinson's shop at number 29 High Street.

Kellett's Doncaster branch shop.

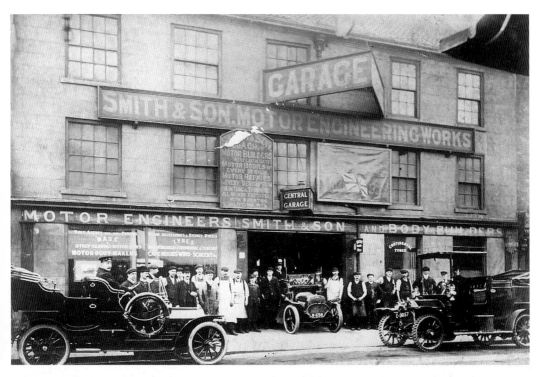

Smith & Son's motor engineering works in St Sepulchre Gate.

Watchmaker, W. Burdett's premises in French Gate.

Charles Mellor's Market Place Doll's Hospital shop was demolished c.1926 due to the Scot Lane widening scheme. He then moved to 55 Hall Gate which was extended in 1952 and 1954 to create more storage space. The shop was sold to Lines Bros in 1959 and was eventually closed.

John Athron, architect and surveyor, was the son of James Athron, a member of the well known firm of Athron & Gill, contractors. John was educated at Jackson's School in Hall Gate and afterwards was associated with his father's firm, but eventually commenced business on his own account in Park Road, pictured here. He died at the early age of 40 in 1911.

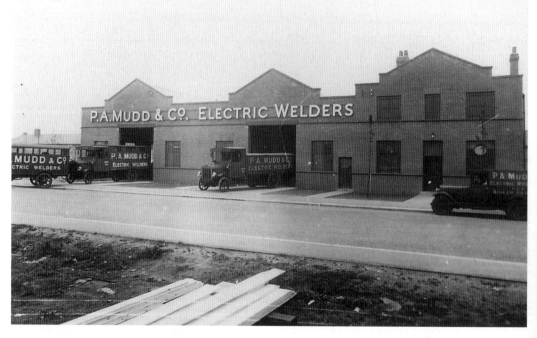

Electrical Welders P.A. Mudd & Co's premises in Leicester Avenue, Intake.

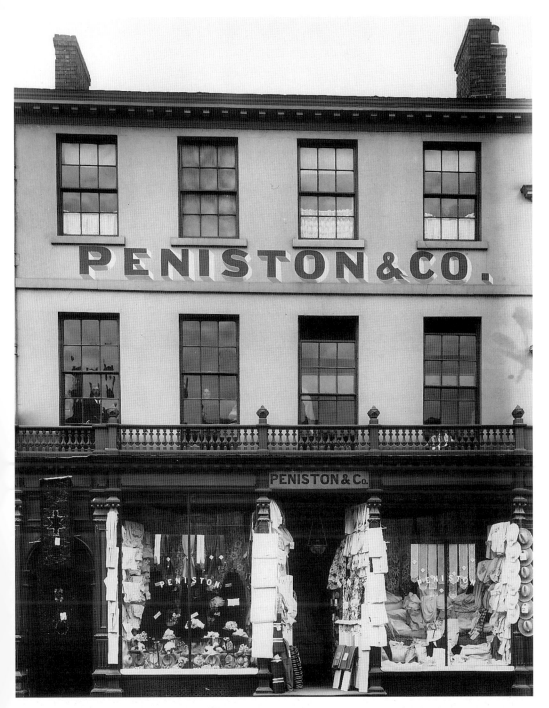

Born in 1816, Edward Peniston came to Doncaster in 1860 and, along with Dennis Roberts, he inaugurated the well-known drapery business, Peniston & Co., in the Market Place. The partnership between Roberts and Peniston only lasted a year, when the latter took control. Roberts eventually set up his own business in St Sepulchre Gate. Edward Peniston, who had lived for some time at Belmont House, Balby Road, died in 1913. He had never taken a very active part in Doncaster's public life.

Stanley Pinder was born in Horbury and was the fourth son of George Pinder who became manager of Doncaster's Lincoln Wagon Works. Stanley commenced his men's outfitting business in St Sepulchre Gate (shown here in both photographs) around 1903. He established branches in Horbury and Wakefield, but later transferred one to a brother and disposed of the other. In the early 1920s, he opened a branch at Bentley, and shortly after another in Printing Office Street. He died in 1930.

Mrs Melbourne's Doncaster branch shop

The Doncaster Rubber Co. Ltd's premises at 32 Baxter Gate.

Slack's Mineral Water Co. Ltd on Balby Road.

Tailor G. Watson's premises at 19 High Street.

Ropemakers Hanson Bros' premises in French Gate. The family's Doncaster history started in 1776 after George Hanson, apprenticed to a rope-maker in Sheffield, decided to settle in Doncaster because his fiancee's family had moved to the town. His fiancee's father had said: "Doncaster is a town where the landed gentry are going to settle because it is a developing market town with plenty of opportunities". It proved true for George, who had learnt his trade well, could write and had a pleasant manner. There were only 11 ropers' stands in Doncaster market. Through six generations the business flourished, unchecked by fires, floods and two world wars.

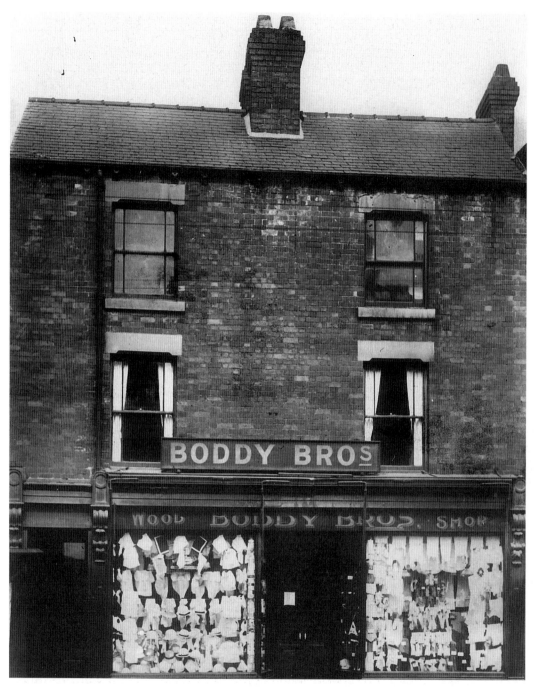

The firm of Boddy Bros was founded as a small shop at 68 St Sepulchre Gate by J.W. Boddy and originally traded in fancy goods. The firm prospered from the start and in 1888 acquired 60 St Sepulchre Gate (pictured here) where a gentleman's outfitting establishment was started. In 1896 a further branch was opened in the Market Place, and this was retained until 1950 when the business was concentrated at 63/65 St Sepulchre Gate. These premises were disposed of during 1953 and acquired by jewellers H. Samuel Ltd.

The City Jewelry Co's premises at 6 Baxter Gate.

Armstrong & Co., general drapers, silk mercers and carpet warehousemen at 13 Baxter Gate, which was erected by John Mirfin in 1826. Following several complicated partnership arrangements, the premises became occupied by Armstrong & Co. around 1892. Later the business was bought by Mr and Mrs G.E. Verity of Pudsey. In 1938, the building was destroyed by fire.

L. Bunting newsagent and tobacconist at 157 Cleveland Street. These premises were situated between John Street and Camden Street.

Edgar Charlesworth established a motorcar business at Wombwell, nr Barnsley during 1913. Later he was helped by his father George Charlesworth. Around 1920, Charleworths, as the firm became known, obtained a Ford franchise. By 1925, the firm was ripe for expansion. Consequently, a site at Bennetthorpe, Doncaster, was developed and occupied in 1926. The operations at Wombwell were closed two years later. During the Second World War, Charlesworths were registered under the Ministry of Supply to carry out essential repairs to vehicles that were specifically needed in the war effort. George Charlesworth died in 1954, aged 83. In 1963, at the time when many other new developments were taking place in the town, Edgar developed the Bennetthorpe site. He died in the following year. His successor was Charles Heely, who had started as an apprentice at Wombwell. This was until 1976 when Christiana, Edgar's only child, took control for a decade. The company is presently run by Tony Charlesworth, Christiana's son by her first marriage. He has adopted his maternal grandfather's surname. The company has recently moved from Bennetthorpe to a site at Barnby Dun.

In 1904 the partnership between Lumley & Postlethwaite was dissolved and the firm of Postlethwaite & Stacey – who were brothers-in-law – came into being. The business, at 16 and 17 Hall Gate, was always directed towards the provision of a complete house furnishing service. Postlethwaite died in 1919, Stacey in 1951, the company being continued by descendants until 1961, when the premises were sold and the site redeveloped.

Henry Cauwood's shop at 127 St James' Street.

Cooplands, perhaps the town's largest and best known family business, has 45 retail outlets and employs some 1,100 people. Scarborough-born Alice Coopland (pictured left) was responsible for setting up the business at 34 Hall Gate (below) during 1931. Alice died in 1953. The Managing Director of the present company is Alice's son David Jenkinson.

David Leesing's pork butcher's shop in Baxter Gate. The building dates from 1894, and whilst Leesing was killed in 1901, successive proprietors kept his name over the shop. The business closed in 1978.

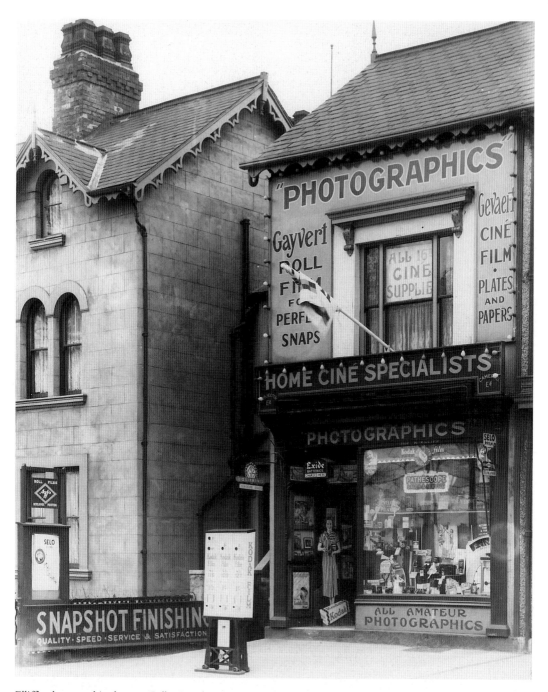

Elliff's photographic shop on Balby Road.

W.E. Clark & Co's premises in Station Road are seen below c.1910, and above in 1942, after bomb damage.

Around 1897, John May established a business at 110 St Sepulchre Gate. In March 1908, he moved to larger premises at 118 and 120 St Sepulchre Gate. These were rebuilt in the 1930s to facilitate street widening. John May died in 1941. The business was then run by George May and his two sons Derek and Jack. The shop suffered bomb damage in 1942. George May died in 1966. Jack retired in 1981, his brother seven years later, and the business closed.

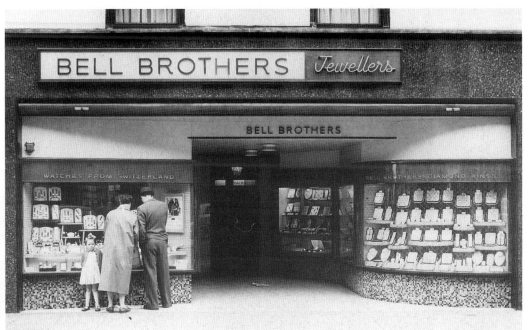

Bell Bros – Doncaster's longest surviving business – 'kicked off' in 1781 and is still thriving today. The firm first had a shop in French Gate, then Baxter Gate, moving to St Sepulchre Gate around 1853. The business remained with the Bell family until 1938, when it was acquired by George Frampton. When the Arndale (now French Gate) Centre was built in the 1960s, Frampton was successful in retaining the freehold of the company's premises.

George Wilton's Victoria Yorkshire Mustard Mills occupied a large area of ground on the south bank of the canal at Marsh Gate. George, born in 1831, had begun the business in the Market Place and transferred it to Marsh Gate in 1867. Large quantities of the company's products were sent all over the world. George Wilton died in 1911. Five months later the company went into voluntary liquidation.

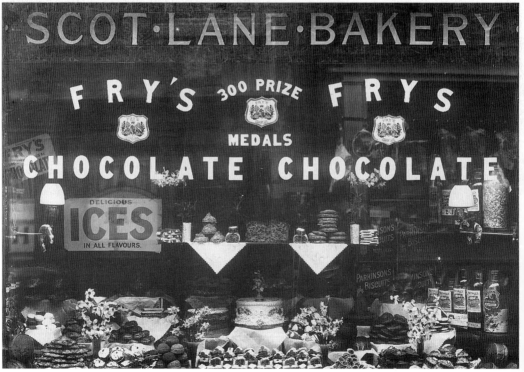

Above: No 39 Hall Gate, now occupied by Francis Sinclair Ltd.

Opposite above: Tobacconist Daniel Portergill spent about 13 years in the premises shown here at the junction of Silver Street/Hall Gate before retiring to Filey in 1912. He died in 1924.

Opposite below: The Scot Lane Bakery.

Ye Olde Curio Shoppe, West Street, now occupied by TAG Models.

Above: Restaurant and provision merchants H. Davy & Son's French Gate property being demolished in the 1960s. This was one of a number which were cleared to make way for the construction of the Arndale (now French Gate) Centre. The building next door but one, on the left, is the White Hart Inn.

Opposite below: J. G. Steadman established himself as a horsebreaker in Silver Street during 1875. Eventually, his business, which became involved with taxis, weddings, and funerals, occupied premises in Highfield Road, and Cleveland Street before moving to Balby Road. Since 1987, the firm has been a part of Hodgson Holdings.

Cutriss's Model Shop, initially called the Cleveland Model Shop, was started c. 1936, in the above premises on Cleveland Street, by Michael Cuttriss, with the assistance of his brother David. Materials were sold for people to make model aeroplanes but, after the War, the shop's popularty soared. This was because the brothers embarked into many different fields including model railways, dinky toys and plastic kits. The business moved a short distance to Duke Street in 1964. Photographs on the right show the interior of the Duke Street shop. Both brothers retired from the business in November 1983.

Left: Seed Merchants Frank Palmer & Sons' shop at 101 St Sepulchre Gate. The property was amongst those demolished in the mid-1960s for the construction of the Inner Relief Road.

Below: Between 1963-1970, Claybourn's service department was accommodated in the above property in Prince's Street. For the next eight years, the sales side of the business was concentrated there.

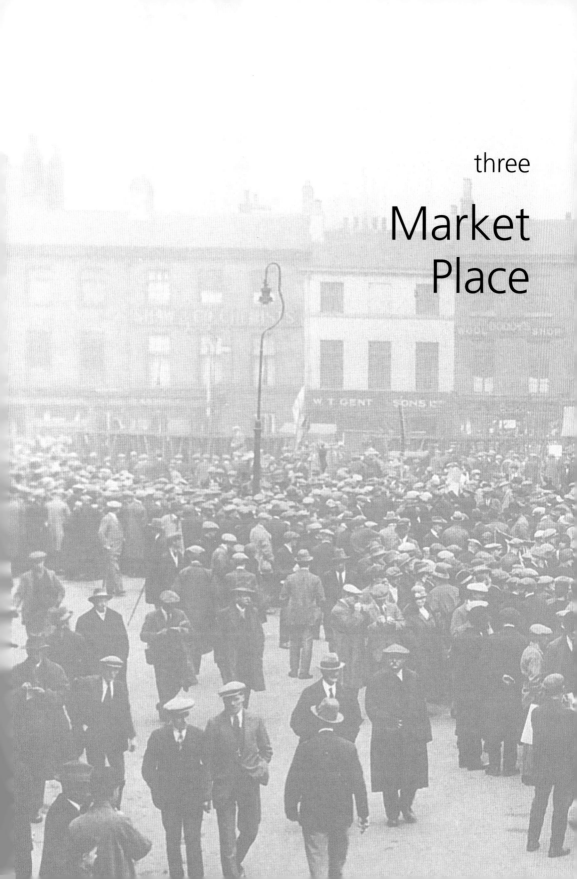

three

Market
Place

A view of the western side of the Market Place looking north.

The south west corner of the Market Place c.1912, with the entrance to Bower's Fold on the extreme right. Noted on the left is the Waverley Commercial Hotel which later moved to St George Gate.

Above: A rear view of the Old Theatre or Royal Opera House in the Market Place, taken c.1899, shortly before its demolition. This was to facilitate further market improvements and alterations.

Right: Market attendant William Duke who remained in harness for 64 years. He died in 1914 aged 84, whilst still an employee of Doncaster Corporation.

The south west side of the Market Place featuring the Woolpack Hotel, which dates back to at least 1707.

Soldiers taking a rest in the Market Place during the First World War.

A 1920s view of the Market Place.

The western side perimeter wall of the Cattle Market extension, which was undertaken in 1908.

Above: Work being carried out on the Cattle Market Extension in 1908. Within the new area, an octagonal auction ring was built. An avenue of trees was also planted on the main driveway in the Cattle Market.

Left: A rear view of the Little Red Lion Inn, which had existed from at least 1793. It was acquired by the Nottingham-based Home Brewery around 1920 and extensively altered eight years later. It was also re-named the Olde Castle Hotel.

Opposite below: Many of the properties in this south west view of the Market Place are still extant today. A notable exception is the Wellington Inn (centre), and today many people feel that its removal from the landscape was unnecessary.

The Cattle Market looking north with High Fisher Gate on the left and Friendly Street running at right angles in the distance. Both thoroughfares were obliterated through redevelopment work during the 1960s.

Above: Tipsters and punters in the Market Place during St Leger Week probably in the late 1920s. The gentleman holding the crowd's attention on the right could be noted tipster Prince Monolulu.

An aerial view of the Market Place looking south during the mid-1920s.

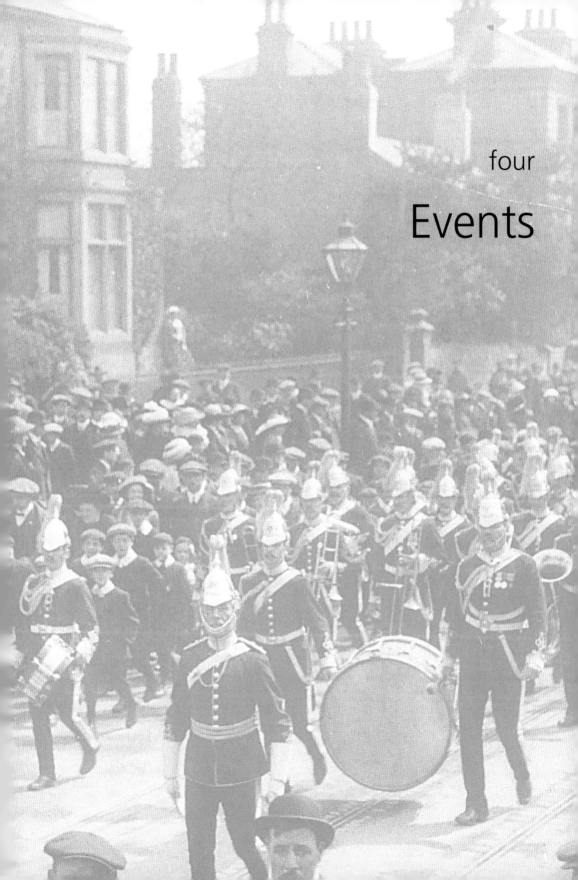

four

Events

Scenes showing a section of the River Cheswold being culveted around 1920.

A military parade passing Albion Place, Bennetthorpe.

The 1919 Peace Celebrations in Wellington Street, Hyde Park.

A Salvation Army Red Cross procession in St Sepulchre Gate.

View of floods May 1932 from the North Bridge.

Two people were badly burned when an explosion ripped through three shops in Holmes Market in November, 1973. The explosion caused by leaking gas demolished a second-hand shop and a fish shop at the junction of Beckett Road and Queen's Road. It also wrecked an adjacent farm produce shop.

five

Buildings

Above: This building was used for some time as a Junior Library and Reading Room before being demolished c.1970 for the second phase of the East By-pass.

Right: The Palace Buffet, built in 1911, adjoined the Palace Theatre (later Essoldo cinema), in Silver Street. It was once the favourite haunt of many music hall stars, including Florrie Forde, G.H. Elliott, Charlie Chaplin, Gertie Gitana, and Frank Randle. It was demolished in the early 1960s.

Opposite above and below: Front and rear views of 49 Hall Gate, which had once been called Moore's cottage, presumably after surgeon John Moore, noted there in 1855. Pictured in the garden here is former Corporation Brewery owner Charles Alfred Ream, with members of his family. The property was demolished during the 1950s.

The Place of Varieties opened in Silver Street during 1911. Live shows were held there until 1920, when it was converted to a cinema. In 1947, it became known as the Essoldo and could accommodate 1,740. It closed in November, 1962.

The Picture House in High Street was opened in 1914, under the auspices of local entrepreneur A.L. Rhodes. Twelve years later, it was taken over by the Associated British Cinema Corporation which once owned over 260 cinemas in Great Britain. The Picture House could provide seating for 1,132 patrons. This continued until closure on 28 October 1967. Two months later, the premises re-opened as a bingo hall.

These properties on the southern side of St Sepulchre Gate are pictured c.1912 shortly before demolition. This was to facilitate the widening of the thoroughfare. The Three Legs public house on the left could be traced back to at least 1782. It was re-named The Yorkist in 1969 and closed 15 years later.

In December 1893, Doncaster Corporation decided to open Sandall Beat Wood to the public as a pleasure ground, between March and October. These two pictures show the woodkeeper's house.

The South Parade Cinema (below) opened in December 1920, but was re-named The Majestic seven years later. It was absorbed by the Gaumont Circuit, during the late 1920s, and was closed in 1933. New premises built on the site were known as the Gaumont Palace (above). This title was held until 1987, when it was changed to the Odeon.

St George's National School was opened, near St George's Church, in June 1868. It was run as a voluntary Church of England School under its own managers until 1961. In subsequent years, the building was demolished in two stages for the construction of the East By-pass.

Mappin's Brewery Office in Friendly Street in 1908.

The Electra in French Gate was Doncaster's first purpose-built picture house. It was extensively altered in 1931 and re-opened, with 'talkies', as the Regal. By the 1950s, it was losing money and closed in 1957. In the following year, it was converted into a clothing store, and finally demolished in the 1960s for the construction of the Arndale (now French Gate) Centre.

six

Yards

Hawksworth's Yard, Duke Street.

Schole's Yard, Portland Place.

Above: Hammond's Yard, Portland Place.

Right: Portland Place from St Sepulchre Gate.

Burton's Yard, Portland Place.

Portland Place.

seven

Aerial
Views

St James' Street looking east. Amongst the houses in the centre are those which formed Oxford Place. Noticeable in the distance is the Chequer Road Museum & Art Gallery under construction.

Opposite above: Taken from St George's Church c.1912, this bird's eye view shows the smoke and grime which once hovered over French Gate. The old Guildhall is on the left. Partly completed on the right is Trafford Street, which was created to give access from the North Bridge to the railway station.

Opposite below: Catherine Street is in the foreground of this view taken from the Council (formerly Coal) House. Beyond is Bentinck Street. Both streets, largely developed during the latter half of the 19th century, were cleared by the early 1970s.

A 1951 view taken over Hyde Park and looking towards the town centre. Some landmarks include the Green Dyke Lane cemetery, on the lower left, and Glasgow Paddocks in Waterdale, just off centre. Over the intervening years much demolition and redevelopment has taken place in the lower half of the picture.

Opposite above: From St George's Church tower c.1961, it may be seen that work has begun, to the left, on the East By-pass. In the middle distance, Jackson's garage, and surrounding properties, were cleared in the mid-1980s for the erection of a supermarket.

Opposite below: Taken from the same location as the previous photograph, this shows the St George Gate/Baxter Gate junction. On the lower right is the Old Library, demolished when the East By-pass was cut through.

Glasgow Paddocks is a prominent feature at the centre of this 1951 view looking east. The route cutting across the photograph from the bottom left hand corner takes in St James' Street, Waterdale and Thorne Road.

We are above the South Parade/Thorne Road junction, in 1934, looking north. The route on the left includes Hall Gate and High Street; the one on the right East Laith Gate and High Fisher Gate.

A 1951 view of Hyde Park looking north. The Green Dyke Lane Cemetery is on the left. The routes converging in the lower half of the picture include Decoy Bank, Middle Bank and Black Bank.

eight

Redevelopment

Looking east at the Spring Gardens/Waterdale junction, where a row of seven terraced properties is being demolished.

A row of properties awaiting demolition in the early 1960s near the Cleveland Street/St Thomas' Street junction.

Work taking place on St Mary's Bridge or Mill Bridge on 1 April 1958. The structure was completed during the following year.

A 1960s shot, taken from Friendly Street, of Ye Olde Crown Inn at the Church Street/Grey Friars' Road corner. The area in the foreground subsequently became the site of Car Park No. 3.

Demolition of cottages adjacent to the Rockingham Arms public house in Bennetthorpe during the 1970s.

Demolition of Hanley's mill during the 1970s. The family's association with the site extended back over a century.

St James' Street, looking east, during redevelopment in the early 1960s.

Cleveland Street at the junction with Baker Street and Duke Street during the early 1960s. All the properties shown were demolished for the development of the Golden Acres site.

The old Museum & Art Gallery, Beechfield House, Waterdale, during demolition in 1963. Viscountess of Halifax opened the Museum in October 1909. The Art Gallery opened a year later.

The new Museum & Art Gallery, Chequer Road, under construction in 1963. The Earl of Rosse had laid the foundation stone in April, 1962.

Following the implementation of the Central Area No. 3 Compulsory Purchase Order, 1959, demolition is nearly complete in Society Street, off Princegate.

A row of shops on the western side of Young Street awaits clearance during the early 1960s.

Two views of the YMCA at the St Sepulchre Gate/Cleveland Street junction showing the building before and during demolition in the 1960s.

Before and after – houses in Waterdale being demolished in the early 1960s for the construction of Copley House.

View from St James' Street looking north west towards the John Street Co-op (left) and the Corporation Brewery, before they suffered the same fate as the other properties in the area.

Houses in Cartwright Street before demolition in the 1960s

Littlewoods basement during excavation in 1972.

Arthur Street looking south in March 1970. All the houses were subsequently demolished, but the school on the left is still extant. The throughfare now forms part of White Rose Way.

Carr House Road, Hyde Park c.1970 before the southern side was demolished for road widening.

Demoliton of the Prince of Wales public house, at the corner of Carr House Road/Wellington Street, Hyde Park, c.1973.

Work on the M18 motorway, near Hatchell Wood (top), and on the Bawtry Road bridge spanning the route, during the 1970s.

Slum clearance in Cemetery Road near the junction with Carr House Road during the early 1970s.

Demolition of the Star Hotel, at the corner of St Jame's Street/Cemetery Road, c.1971.

Clearance of properties in East Laithe Gate during the early 1980s.

Properties in Marsh Gate awaiting demolition during the 1970s.

The construction of the concrete bridge over the main London–Edinburgh railway line, was carried out during the mid–1970s by Retford-based contractors A.F. Budge Ltd.

Demolition of the Bridge Hotel, Marsh Gate, during the early 1970s.

This is really a before and after sequence, as the North Bridge bus station, under construction in the top photograph, now covers much of the area depicted in the older view.

View from Factory Lane showing demolition in Station Road during the early 1970s. This was for the construction of the second phase of the Arndale (now French Gate) Centre.

House clearance on the northern side of Cleveland Street, near the junction with Duke Street, during the early 1960s.

Shown from Bradford Row, much of the property seen on East Laith Gate, has been cleared and the site now provides a car park.

Pell's Close, shown here looking east, was absorbed in the construction of the Colonnades, during the mid–1980s. However, a link between, Printing Office Street and Duke Street, once provided by the thoroughfare, was incorporated in the development.

The Roman Catholic Church of St Peter-in-Chains in Prince's Street, was completed in 1867, to the designs of Sheffield architects Messr Hadfield & Son. Red bricks with stone dressings were used in the construction of the building, and it was erected on the site of a previous chapel and school, also dedicated to St Peter. The picture here shows a large 'rose' window and two lancet windows at the front over the main entrance. Also to be seen is the bell turret. St Peter's was demolished during the 1970s. A new church built in Chequer Road took the same name.

Clearance of the old Doncaster Evening Post site on North Bridge during November, 1988.

Built c.1915, the Elephant Hotel on St Sepulchre Gate is seen shortly before demolition in the mid-1970s. The site is currently occupied by the Yorkshire Bank PLC.

Many of these St Sepulchre Gate properties were demolished for the construction of the Inner Relief Road in the mid-1960s.

Scaffolding going up round the old *Doncaster Gazette* office in Printing Office where demolition work started in February, 1980. The premises had stood empty for 13 years.

Houses on Green Dyke Lane which were demolished, amidst heated protests from the occupants in the mid-1970s for the construction of a dual carriageway.

French Gate looking towards Clock Corner c.1961, where work had just commenced on demolishing some of the properties for the construction of the East By-pass.

Taken from one of the high-rise flats during the late 1960s, this features, in the foreground, the Turf Tavern at the junction of St James' Street and Bentinck Street. The Coal (now Council) House is under construction in the background.